*A Victorian Childhood*

# At School

# Ruth Thomson

W
FRANKLIN WATTS
LONDON•SYDNEY

First published in 2007 by Franklin Watts
338 Euston Road, London NW1 3BH

Franklin Watts Australia
Hachette Children's Books
Level 17/207 Kent Street
Sydney NSW 2000

**Designer:** Mei Lim
**Editor:** Susie Brooks

The author would like to thank John and Sandy Howarth
of Swiss Cottage Antiques, Leeds and Islington Education
Library Service (www.objectlessons.org) for the loan of
items from their collections.

**Photographic acknowledgements**
Neil Thomson: 1, 2, 4b, 5c, 6, 7, 8t, 9, 10, 13, 14, 15tl, 16cl,
17br and bl, 18tr and bl, 26, 27; London Metropolitan
Archives: cover, 8b, 12b, 15b, 16b, 18t, 21t, 22b, 23b, 25tr;
Peter Millard/The Jill Grey Collection, Hitchin British
Schools/ Franklin Watts Picture Library 19b, 20t; Mary
Evans Picture Library 24c.

A CIP catalogue record for this book is available from
the British Library.

Dewey Classification: 371'.00941

ISBN 978 0 7496 7049 8

Printed and bound in Malaysia

Franklin Watts is a division of Hachette Children's Books.

# Contents

# EARLY SCHOOLS

It is hard to imagine now, but when Queen Victoria came to the throne in 1837, there was no law that said children had to go to school.

Governess ▲

## Learning or work

Most rich and middle class boys went to private schools, which charged **fees**, but girls and young boys were generally taught at home by a **governess**. Many poor children did not go to school at all. They worked from an early age to earn much-needed money for their families. Some children learned to read and write at the factory where they worked.

Many churches and chapels had Sunday schools which taught children to read so they could learn about the Bible. Some of them also ran schools during the week.

Sunday and Infant School.

Moses  Noah  Obadiah

Peter  Queen Esther  Rebekah

Even alphabet books were based on the Bible.

## Schools for the poor

In villages, some young children went to a Dame school where an old woman – the 'dame' – taught them in her own home.

In poor areas of big cities, hundreds of ragged schools gave free schooling to very poor and often homeless children. The author Charles Dickens described these children as 'too ragged, wretched, filthy and forlorn' to enter any other place.

Children learned basic reading and writing at a Dame school. Parents paid a few pence each week.

The first ragged schools were set up in disused stables, lofts and railway arches. They often provided food and shelter as well as schooling.

▲ Victorian pennies

FIELD LANE RAGGED SCHOOL

# SCHOOLS FOR ALL

In 1870, **Parliament** passed a **law** called the Education Act that said school places should be available for all children up to the age of ten.

## Board schools

Groups of people were elected on to **School Boards** to set up new schools in their area. These were paid for by the rates (a local tax). Hundreds of new Board Schools were built, particularly in towns and cities. These huge, impressive buildings towered above the surrounding houses. Some had as many as 1,000 pupils. Parents had to pay a few pence a week for their children to attend until 1891, when schooling was made free.

## Boys, girls and infants

Infants – aged 5 to 7 – were taught on the ground floor. After the age of 7, boys and girls were taught separately. Boys' classrooms were on the first floor and girls' classrooms were on the top floor. Boys and girls had separate playgrounds with a high wall between them. Some schools in built-up areas also had a playground on the roof.

Boys and girls had separate entrances, often marked in stone above the gate.

6

## Look out for these features of Board Schools:

- two or more floors
- large, tall windows
- school board, school name and date plaques
- chimneys for the coal-fired stoves that heated classrooms on very cold days
- a high surrounding wall or railings
- separate entrances for boys, girls and infants
- playgrounds surrounded by high brick walls

Few people owned clocks or watches. A bell rang to tell children it was time for school to start.

# THE CLASSROOM

Classrooms were crowded with up to 60 children. The huge windows let in as much light as possible, and gaslamps were lit on gloomy days. High ceilings helped to **ventilate** the room and let gas fumes escape.

How does your classroom compare with this one?

- How are the desks arranged?
- Where does your teacher sit?
- What equipment do you use?
- What is on the walls?
- What does the teacher write on?

## The classroom layout

Children sat at desks, arranged in long rows, facing the teacher's desk at the front. The floor was stepped so that children in the back rows could see the blackboard and the teacher, and the teacher could keep an eye on the whole class at once.

## Desks and benches

The wooden benches and desks were screwed to the floor. Hinged flaps on the desks could be raised for reading lessons and laid flat for writing on. Notice the slot for storing a slate, the inkwell, the shelf underneath for books and the sloping foot rest.

◀ Slate

Inkwell ▶

## The pupils

Pupils had to sit still with straight backs, with their hands on their laps or behind their backs, if they were listening to the teacher. They were not allowed to talk unless a teacher asked them a question.

# THE SCHOOL DAY

**S**chool started at 9 o'clock prompt. Children lined up in their class groups in the playground and went into a large hall for assembly.

The children sang a hymn, said prayers and listened to a Bible reading at assembly.

## Important lessons

Schools wanted to make sure that children became good Christians. The first lesson for every class each day was scripture – all about the Bible. On Fridays, pupils had **catechism,** where they learned answers to questions about their religion. Most of each day then concentrated on the 3Rs – Reading and wRiting and aRithmetic.

Children took it in turns to read aloud a paragraph from the class reading book. Many of the stories had moral messages which showed how to behave well.

The teacher showed children how to do sums on a big **abacus** like this.

## TIMETABLE

| Time | Monday | Tuesday | Wednesday | Thursday | Friday |
|------|--------|---------|-----------|----------|--------|
| 9.00 – 9.15 | *PRAYERS AND SINGING* | | | | |
| 9.15 – 9.50 | *Scripture* | *Scripture* | *Scripture* | *Scripture* | *Catechism* |
| 9.50 – 10.00 | *REGISTER* | | | | |
| 10.00 – 11.00 | *Arithmetic* | *Arithmetic* | *Arithmetic* | *Arithmetic* | *Arithmetic* |
| 11.00 – 11.10 | *RECREATION (playtime)* | | | | |
| 11.10 – 12.00 | *Reading* | *Reading* | **Dictation** | *Reading* | *Reading* |
| 12.00 – 2.00 | *LUNCHTIME* | | | | |
| 2.00 – 2.10 | *REGISTER* | | | | |
| 2.10 – 3.00 | *Dictation* | *Dictation (Girls sew for 2 hours)* | *Reading* | *Dictation* | *Dictation (Girls sew for 2 hours)* |
| 3.00 – 3.30 | *Mental arithmetic* | *Geography* | **Recitation** | *Singing* | *Geography* |
| 3.30 – 4.10 | *Writing* | *Writing* | *Writing* | *Writing* | *Writing* |

## Time for lunch

There was a long break at lunchtime, because there were no school dinners. Some children went home to eat. Others brought bread and cheese with them, if it was too far for them to walk home. **Charities** sometimes gave bread and soup to the poorest children who would otherwise have gone hungry.

How does this 1872 timetable compare with yours?

- Which subjects are the same as yours and which are different?
- What extra lesson did girls have?
- How much play time was there?

At the end of the day, children knelt at their desks and the teacher said a prayer.

# LEARNING TO WRITE

**P**upils all learned the same thing at the same time. They copied down, word for word, what the teacher wrote on the blackboard or read out to them.

▲ Sand tray

The children learned to write the alphabet one letter at a time.

## Drawing in sand

Infants learned to write by drawing letters in a tray of sand. They drew in the sand with their fingers. The sand could be smoothed over and used again.

## Slates

Once children knew their letters, they wrote on slates with a thin slate pencil. Paper was costly, but slates could be wiped clean and used again. Children were supposed to use a damp rag to clean their slate, but most used spit and their sleeve instead.

▲ Slate and slate pencil

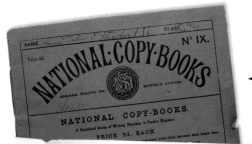

◄ Copybook with **proverbs**

## Copybooks

Older children used pen and ink. They copied sentences printed in a copybook word for word. Pupils all wrote exactly the same way, in a sloping style known as **copperplate**.

Teachers gave dictation. Children had to write down what the teacher read out, spelling tricky words correctly.

The split steel pen nibs often got crossed and dripped ink. Children were punished if they made ink blots in their copybooks.

### Dictation exercise

I **know no** one who does not like **new** clothes.

He thought he **knew** more than any one else.

Then they **knew** it was of **no** use to **know** that.

Do you **know** now how I **knew** those were not **new**?

We **know no new** way to learn to read.

# OTHER SUBJECTS

Once Board Schools were well established, more interesting lessons were introduced.

Blacksmith ▼

## Object lessons

Infant children had object lessons. The teacher held up an object or a picture and asked children questions about it. Some object lessons were about common things such as a bird's egg, a lead pencil, a candle or an apple. Others were about more unusual topics, such as horsehair, glue, whalebone, a railway carriage or a blacksmith's shop.

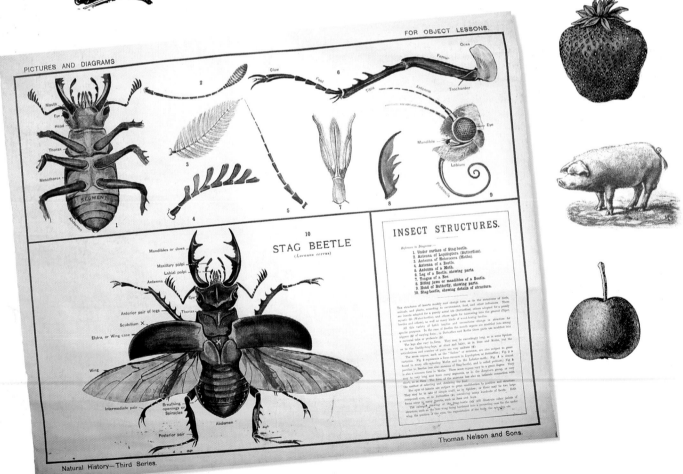

▲ Chart for object lessons

## Skills for jobs

Some older children went to schools where they learned useful skills. Boys learned printing, shoemaking and tailoring. Girls went to a house-wifery centre where they learned how to lay a fire, clean and polish a house, darn and patch clothes, to do the **laundry** and look after babies.

Boys learned how to make shoes and clothes by hand.

## Special schools

By the end of Victoria's reign, children who were blind, deaf or disabled could go to special schools.

Blind boys learned useful skills for jobs, such as basket making, chair caning, mat making and sewing.

# BOYS' LESSONS

The Victorians thought that boys should be taught useful skills for jobs they might have in the future. In the afternoons, the older boys at Board Schools had different lessons from girls.

◄ Drawing copybook

## Drawing class

Boys were taught to draw in a precise, technical way. They learned to draw by copying simple shapes, patterns and objects printed in a drawing copybook. Then they practised drawing objects, such as pyramids, cones, cubes and vases, arranged on a table in front of them. Everyone's drawings looked much the same.

Later, boys learned to make working drawings for their woodwork models.

Workshops were light, airy and well equipped.

## Workshops

From 1885, workshops known as Manual Training Centres were built in the playground of many Board Schools. Older boys learned to use woodwork tools, such as those shown on the right, to help them become skilled with their hands. Some boys also learned gardening.

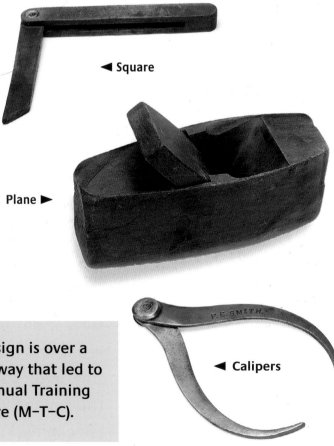

◄ Square

Plane ►

◄ Calipers

This sign is over a doorway that led to a Manual Training Centre (M–T–C).

# GIRLS' LESSONS

The Victorians thought girls should know how to be good housewives and mothers, so schools taught girls home-making skills.

By the time girls left school, they had learned to make petticoats, nightshirts, a girl's frock and a man's shirt.

Girls practised their stitching by making miniature clothes before they made real ones.

## Sewing skills

It was thought to be essential to teach girls needlework, so they knew how to make and mend clothes. Girls spent four hours a week learning to stitch, hem, seam and make buttonholes. They had to sew with tiny, even stitches. Mistakes had to be unpicked and the sewing done again. Once a year, an examiner checked what the girls had made.

## Cookery

Older girls learned cookery, and how to shop for food, at Cookery Centres built in the grounds of some schools.

## Laundry work

There were no washing machines in Victorian times, so girls learned how to wash and **starch** clothes by hand. They also practised using different sorts of irons.

A cookery lesson ▼

Wash board for scrubbing clothes against ▼

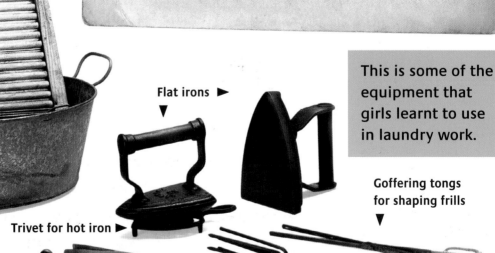

Soap ▲

An extract from a textbook on laundry work

WASH DAY
Rise early! We can do more in one hour in the early morning than in two in the afternoon. The air is fresher and contains less smoke and dust and we are stronger. Light the boiler fire and a good supply of hot water.
1st Get out the dirt. Soak, wash, ie rub and rinse well.
2nd Keep everything a good colour. To keep the colour in white things, boil, blue and dry in the open air. To keep the colour in coloured things, wash and dry quickly.

This is some of the equipment that girls learnt to use in laundry work.

Flat irons ▶
▼

Goffering tongs for shaping frills
▼

Trivet for hot iron ▶

Clothes pegs ▶

# EXERCISE AND HYGIENE

At fee-paying schools with large grounds, pupils played team sports, such as rugby, football and cricket. At Board Schools, which had small playgrounds, the only exercise children did was drill.

▲ Dumb-bells

Once a year, some schools performed a drill display at the Royal Albert Hall in London.

## Drill

During drill, pupils lined up in rows in the playground and a teacher shouted commands. The children had to jump, bend or stretch in perfect time together. Sometimes, they lifted clubs or dumb-bells. Teachers thought that drill was a good way of teaching children how to obey orders, as well as giving them exercise.

In cold weather, boys wore their jackets and caps for drill.

This teacher is checking children's scalps for **ringworm**. Children with dirty heads, sores, or rashes were sent home, so they did not infect the others.

## Keeping clean

Poor pupils often came to school unwashed and in dirty clothes. The teachers' first job every day was to make sure children's hands and faces were clean and that they were not showing any signs of illness.

## Health and illness

Poor children often had sore eyes, matted hair and rotten teeth. They rarely owned hairbrushes or toothbrushes. Small, weak and underfed, these children easily caught diseases, such as smallpox, diphtheria, typhoid and scarlet fever, that are much rarer now. Some died. During an **epidemic**, a school was closed, sometimes for weeks. Headteachers kept a record of illnesses in a **log book**.

### Log book entries

*September 2*
Several children absent through whooping cough in the house.
*September 9*
A great deal of sickness prevails, especially measles.
*November 10*
A few cases of scarlet fever.

Have you or any of your classmates had any of these illnesses?

21

# ABSENCES

When Board Schools first started, it was hard to persuade poor parents to send their children to school. They needed children to work. Until schools became free, many families could not afford or refused to pay for schooling.

## Mini-mothers
Girls often stayed at home on washday or to look after their brothers and sisters.

▲ Reward card

Headteachers encouraged pupils to be punctual by giving Reward cards to those who turned up on time all term.

Pupils who attended school regularly were rewarded with book prizes.

Which of these reasons for absence might still be accepted today?

## Attendances

School Boards paid a **grant** to schools for every day that a child attended. If attendance was low, schools received less money. Head-teachers were keen to make sure children came to school regularly. They had to keep a record of weekly attendance in their log book, which was inspected once a year.

## Attendance officers

School Boards hired attendance officers to track down children who should have been at school.

### Log book entries

*January 13*
Attendance affected by dense fog.

*February 22-27*
Attendance exceedingly low, affected by a severe snowstorm. Many of our children are ill booted, clothed and fed.

*April 26-May 3*
The fine weather of the past week seems to keep down attendance in the upper class.

*May 9*
Frequently the boys who play truant go into the park to pick up the ball for the gentlemen playing cricket. Others go about picking up iron to sell at the marine stove dealer.

*June 28*
Several were absent this week owing to hay-making having commenced.

*July 5*
Several Sunday school treats this week have interfered with the attendance of many children.

*August 23*
Several girls are still in the country and a few have gone hop picking.

Pupils who never missed a single day at school for several years running were rewarded with Queen Victoria medals.

# PUNISHMENTS AND REWARDS

**T**eachers tried to make pupils work hard, behave well and arrive on time by being very strict. Pupils were usually very scared of their fierce teachers.

**Cane ▶**

## Being caned

Children who talked or laughed in class, made spelling mistakes, ink blots or disobeyed the teacher were beaten with a thin, bendy birch **cane**.

## Punishment book

Headteachers kept a record of canings in a punishment book. Girls were caned only across the hand. Boys were often caned across their bottoms.

▲ Boy wearing a dunce's cap – a punishment for poor work

## Punishment book entries

| Name of child | Age | Offence | Punishment |
|---|---|---|---|
| Kathleen Scott | 9 | Disobedience | 2 strokes |
| Elizabeth Kybert | 9 | Lying | 4 strokes |
| Ada Horne | 13 | Impertinence | 4 strokes |
| Rose Harwood | 7 | Laziness and temper | 2 strokes |
| Beatrice Lewis | 8 | Continual lateness | 2 strokes |
| Mabel Archer | 10 | Obstinacy | 3 strokes |
| Edith Turner | 9 | Talking and playing | 4 strokes |
| Florence Cook | 8 | Whistling in class | 2 strokes |
| Florence Gray | 8 | Truanting | 6 strokes |
| Kathleen Scott | 9 | Vulgarity | 2 strokes |
| May Piggott | 9 | Scribbling in book | 2 strokes |
| May Reed | 8 | Cheating | 2 strokes |
| Louisa Jones | 10 | Playing with gas | 4 strokes |
| Elsie Scott | 13 | Careless work | 1 stroke |
| Bertha Gooby | 8 | Eating in school | 2 strokes |
| Alice Staines | 7 | Playing with ink | 1 stroke |
| Nelly Harwood | 8 | Very untidy work | 1 stroke |

**Compare these entries in a punishment book.**

- Were pupils punished more for bad behaviour or for poor work?
- What was considered the worst offence of all?

## Yearly inspections

An **inspector** visited schools once a year to test children on reading, writing and arithmetic. Children had to pass these tests to move up from one class or **Standard** to another.

## Payment by results

It was important for teachers that the pupils did well. If the test results were bad, the school grant was cut and so were teachers' wages. Teachers drilled children to answer exact questions and remember everything they learned off by heart.

▼ School certificate

## Certificates and books

Children who passed the tests were rewarded with certificates and book prizes. Some schools gave children a half day's holiday for good results.

## Rewards and treats

School was not all hard work, especially on Friday afternoons and at the end of term. Children went on outings to the zoo, the country or to a park. Sometimes they had a magic lantern show or extra playtime.

This teacher is giving a book prize to a star pupil.

# FINDING OUT MORE

**D**o your own project on Victorian schools. Compare a Victorian classroom, lessons, rules and equipment with those in your own school.

## Looking at buildings

Some Victorian school buildings are still in use as schools. Others have been turned into offices, homes, studios or community centres. Find your nearest Victorian school and do some detective work.

What sorts of schools were there in your local area in Victorian times? Find out when they were built.

How have Victorian schools changed? Have any new buildings been added? Are the entrances still the same?

Some Victorian schools are now houses. How have they been altered? What features show they were once a school?

Look for other clues of old schools, such as a school bell, a plaque on a house or the name of a road.

**RULES AND REGULATIONS**
FOR THE
ASHBY-DE-LA-ZOUCH
**INFANTS' SCHOOL.**

I. Infants are received into this School at the age of eighteen months.

II. The day for admission is every Monday morning, between the hours of nine and ten.

III. No child can be admitted without bringing a written order from the Rev. M. Vavasour, or some other Subscriber.

IV. The School will commence at Nine o'clock in the morning, and at Two in the afternoon. The children are allowed to bring their dinner and remain in the Master's care till Four o'clock in the winter, and in summer till Five.

V. Children must attend punctually at the hour of school, and come with their hands and faces clean washed, and their hair neatly cut and combed.

VI. Any parent who allows a child to attend the School knowing or suspecting that it has any symptoms of infectious disorders, such as hooping cough, scarlet fever, or the like, will be liable to forfeit ... establishment, and to have his child finally excluded. ...hildren at home, on account of sickness, or he ... the Master accordingly.

## Documents and photographs

The Record Office of your nearest County Archives Department holds school log books, admission registers, minutes of School Board meetings, certificates, old photographs and prints. Local museums, history societies and libraries can also be useful sources of information.

Children dressed smartly for photographs. Notice their clothes and footwear. Can you spot any medals? Look for a board saying which Standard the photo shows.

## Old books

Second-hand bookshops may have old school books or stories about Victorian school life. Books often give fascinating information about what schools were like and what pupils learned.

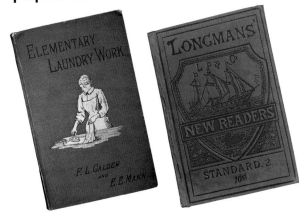

### Extract from a Geography book

Great Britain, the largest island in Europe, is divided into England, Scotland and Wales. It is about 600 miles long and 250 broad.

The climate of England is extremely variable, but in general healthy; the soil is fertile and in the highest state of cultivation.

England abounds in mineral productions, particularly tin, lead, iron and coal; the last two of which greatly contribute to the flourishing state of her manufactures.

The population of England in 1881 was upward of 24,608,000.

# TIMELINE

## 1830s

**1837** Victoria came to the throne.

## 1840s

**1844** The Ragged Schools Union was set up.

**1844** A Law was passed saying children in factories had to have 6 half days of schooling per week.

**1846** A Pupil-teacher system was started in schools. Older pupils called monitors were used as teachers.

## 1870s

**1870** The Education Act allowed School Boards to set up Board Schools.

**1871** Schools were encouraged to include drill in their timetable.

**1874** A Factory Act raised the minimum working age to 9 years.

**1875** Cookery lessons were added to the school timetable.

## 1890s

**1891** Boys' drawing lessons were added to the timetable.

**1891** Schooling was made free.

**1891** A Factory Act raised the minimum working age to 11.

**1892** A Shop Hours Act limited working hours for under 18s to 74 hours a week.

**1893** The school leaving age was raised to 11.

## 1850s

**1851** Almost two million children went to Sunday School, according to the 1851 census.

**1857** The Industrial Schools Act was passed. Schools were set up for neglected and homeless children who might turn to crime.

## 1860s

**1862** 'Payment by results' started. Grants given to schools now depended on how well pupils did in their annual exams.

**1862** Headteachers were required to keep log books of details about attendance, illness, visitors, exams and teachers.

## 1880s

**1880** Schooling for children between the ages of 5 and 10 was made compulsory.

**1882** The London Board School Free Dinner Fund was launched.

**1882** A new Standard VII was introduced for children who wanted to stay at school beyond the minimum leaving age.

**1887** Queen Victoria's Golden Jubilee (50 years on the throne) took place.

**1887** Queen Victoria medals for perfect attendance were introduced.

## 1900s

**1894** The Prevention of Cruelty to Children Act was passed. Children under 11 were not allowed to perform or sell in the street.

**1895** Object lessons were made compulsory for infants.

Visits to zoo, museums and other places were encouraged.

**1897** Queen Victoria's Diamond Jubilee (60 years on the throne) took place.

**1899** The school leaving age was raised to 12 years.

**1901** Queen Victoria died.

# GLOSSARY

**abacus** a counting frame with coloured balls that move along wires

**cane** a stick used to beat a child

**catechism** questions and answers about Christianity which pupils had to learn by heart

**charity** an organisation that helps and raises money for good causes, such as the poor or the environment

**copperplate** a style of writing in thin, sloping, looped letters

**dictation** a passage that teachers read aloud for children to write down

**epidemic** when many people catch a disease or illness at the same time

**fee** an amount of money that someone pays for a service, such as education

**governess** a woman employed by a family to teach children in their own home

**grant** a sum of money given, often by the government, for a particular purpose

**inspector** a government official who tested how well pupils and teachers were doing

**laundry** washing clothes, bedding and other things

**law** a rule made by Parliament that everyone must obey

**log book** a school diary in which the headteacher filled in details of what happened at school each day

**Parliament** the place where elected MPs (Members of Parliament) meet to discuss and make laws for the country

**proverb** a short sentence that gives advice or expresses a truth

**recitation** saying something, such as a poem, out loud

**ringworm** a skin disease caused by a type of fungus

**School Board** a group of people who set up and ran Board Schools

**starch** a powder used to make clean clothes stiff, so they did not crease

**Standard** the name for different school years in Victorian schools, such as Standard II

**ventilate** to let fresh air into a room or building

# PLACES TO VISIT

All the places below include either a real or reconstructed Victorian school room. Most of them run living history role-play lessons where you can experience what it was like to be a Victorian schoolchild.

**The Black Country Living Museum**
Tipton Road, Dudley, West Midlands DY1 4SQ
www.bclm.co.uk

**Blists Hill Victorian Town, Ironbridge Gorge Museums**
Legges Way, Madeley, Telford, Shropshire TF7 5DU
www.ironbridge.org.uk

**Bradford Industrial Museum**
Moorside Road, Bradford, W. Yorkshire BD2 3HP
www.bradfordmuseums.org/bim

**Braintree District Museum**
Market Place, Braintree, Essex CM7 3YG
www.enjoybraintreedistrict.co.uk/museum

**Brewhouse Yard Museum**
Castle Boulevard, Nottingham, NG7 1FB
www.nottinghamcity.gov.uk/sitemap/brewhouse_yard

**The British Schools Museum**
41/42 Queen Street, Hitchin, Hertfordshire SG4 9TS
www.hitchinbritishschools.org.uk

**Helston Folk Museum**
Market Place, Helston, Cornwall TR13 8TH
www.kerrier.gov.uk

**Katesgrove Schoolroom**
Dorothy Street, Reading, Berkshire RG1 2NL
www.katesgrove-schoolroom.org

**Leeds Industrial Museum**
Armley Mills, Canal Road, Armley, Leeds LS12 2QF
www.leeds.gov.uk/armleymills

**Macclesfield Heritage Centre**
Roe Street, Macclesfield, Cheshire SK11 6UT
www.silk-macclesfield.org

**Milton Keynes Museum**
McConnell Drive, Wolverton, Milton Keynes MK12 5EL
www.mkmuseum.org.uk/exhibit/school.htm

**Museum of English Rural Life**
Redlands Road, Reading, Berkshire RG1 5EX
www.reading.ac.uk/Instits/im

**North of England Open Air Museum**
Beamish, County Durham DH9 0RG
www.beamish.org.uk

**Park Hall Farm**
Oswestry, Shropshire SY11 4AS
www.parkhallfarm.co.uk

**Radstock Museum**
Waterloo Road, Radstock, Bath, Avon BA3 3ER
www.radstockmuseum.co.uk

**Ragged School Museum**
46-50 Copperfield Road, London E3 4RR
www.raggedschoolmuseum.org.uk

**St Fagans National History Museum (Wales)**
St Fagans, Cardiff CF5 6XB
www.museumwales.ac.uk/en/stfagans

**Scotland Street School Museum**
225 Scotland Street, Glasgow G5 8QB
www.glasgowmuseums.com

**Sevington Victorian School**
Sevington, Grittleton, Chippenham, Wiltshire SN14 7LD
www.sevingtonvictorianschool.co.uk

**Shugborough Historic Estate**
Milford, near Stafford ST17 0XB
www.shugborough.org.uk

**Sudbury Hall – The National Trust Museum of Childhood**
Sudbury Hall, Ashbourne, Derbyshire DE6 5HT
www.nationaltrust.org.uk

**Ulster Folk and Transport Museum**
Cultra, Holywood, Co. Down, Northern Ireland BT18 0EU
www.uftm.org.uk

**Weald and Downland Open Air Museum**
Singleton, Chichester, West Sussex, PO18 0EU
www.wealddown.co.uk

**Wigan Pier Heritage Centre**
Wallgate, Wigan, Lancashire WN3 4EU
www.wlct.org/tourism/wiganpier/wiganpier.htm

# INDEX

**These are the lists of contents for each title in** *A Victorian Childhood:*

**At Home**
The move to towns • Homes for poor people • Suburbs • Comfortable homes • Heat and light • Washing and baths • Families • Babies • Health and illness • Clothes • Keeping in touch

**At Play**
The nursery • Indoor play • Pastimes • Sundays • Outdoor fun • Sports • Street games • Entertainment • Outings • Holidays • The Seaside

**At School**
Early schools • Schools for all • The classroom • The school day • Learning to write • Other subjects • Boys' lessons • Girls' lessons • Exercise and hygiene • Absences • Punishments and rewards

**At Work**
Child workers • Nasty jobs • On the farm • In the home • Cottage industries • Shop boys • Street sellers • Guttersnipes • Scavengers • Helping children • Schools